yes, Lord
"Take My Life"
Joyce Watson

"Take My Life"

The Essence of a
Christian's Response to God

by
Audrey J. Williamson

Beacon Hill Press of Kansas City
Kansas City, Missouri

Printed in the United States of America

ISBN: 0-8341-0812-7

Cover Art: Crandall Vail

Permission to quote from the following copyrighted versions of the Bible
is acknowledged with appreciation:

The Holy Bible, New International Version (NIV), copyright © 1978 by
New York International Bible Society.

From the *New Testament in Modern English* (Phillips), Revised Edition
© J. B. Phillips 1958, 1960, 1972. By permission of the Macmillan
Publishing Co., Inc.

If He is truly on the throne,
then He will keep our hearts ablaze.
Take your heart's temperature. If
it is low, do something about it!

TAKE MY LIFE

Take my life, and let it be
Consecrated, Lord, to Thee.

Take my moments and my days,
Let them flow in ceaseless praise.

Take my hands, and let them move
At the impulse of Thy love.

Take my feet, and let them be
Swift and beautiful for Thee.

Take my voice, and let me sing
Always, only, for my King.

Take my lips, and let them be
Filled with messages for Thee.

Take my silver and my gold;
Not a mite would I withhold.

Take my intellect, and use
Every power as Thou shalt choose.

Take my will and make it Thine;
It shall be no longer mine.

Take my heart; it is Thine own!
It shall be Thy royal throne.

Take my love; my God, I pour
At Thy feet its treasure store.

Take myself and I will be
Ever, only, all for Thee.

—FRANCES RIDLEY HAVERGAL

I have known these verses since childhood. And now, as I recall how often my husband quoted them in his speaking and writing, they take on even greater importance. Since his "release" the couplets have become the basis of the devotional outline we share together in this book.

Audrey J. Williamson

No reservations
No withholdings
No Bargaining
wholly his own
Constantly, Exclusively, Completely
His — Ever, only,
all for Thee

"Take My Life"

In this opening phrase of Frances Ridley Havergal's immortal hymn, lies the essence of the true Christian response to all that God affords us in Calvary's redemption, forgiveness, cleansing, infilling, and God's enabling presence; all ours even now.

As this Spirit-directed, saintly hymnist explores the full concept of entire consecration, she reaches into every area of our lives. She makes holiness of heart and life a normal experience and the divine standard for all our daily living.

Surely Dr. Audrey J. Williamson was divinely inspired to search out these beautiful and probing lines for her latest "sublime truth series." Throughout the entire series of morning devotionals during the Laymen's Retreat, her own warmth of spirit shone through and seemed to say, "This I believe and have found to be true." As usual, she searched out the Word of God for herself and quoted verbatim soul-refreshing scripture passages again and again. Now the hundreds who heard her may peruse these pages and recapture something of the glow of those blessed hours.

Our deepest desire is that those who were unable to attend the retreat will find a quiet time to read these pages for themselves and feel something of the same divine lift.

Our sincere prayer is that these pages will reach around the world, even to faraway places, where our church and her servants serve with joy and gladness in telling the story of Jesus and His love. With a united voice, let us sing again from our hearts today:

Take my life and let it be
Consecrated, Lord, to Thee!

VERNON E. LUNN, *Chairman*
International Laymen's Conference
Church of the Nazarene

I

Take my LIFE, and let it be Consecrated, Lord, to Thee.

My life, God? Take my life? My very being? My most precious possession? The very essence of my existence? Dearer to me even than health; that to which I cling even when health is gone? Dearer to me than any possession? More precious than any achievement? And I should voluntarily say, "Take my life"? But why? I shall have nothing left!

My life is housed in this body, so when I give You my life, I am giving You my body. My hands and feet, my eyes and ears, my mind, my total personality. The living me is controlled by my body and all its members and functions. If I give You my life, I am surrendering my body as well. It will pass from my possession to Your possession.

And this is just what God desires—what Paul enjoined us to do in Rom. 12:1-2: "I beg you," he says (there is urgency in this appeal), "I beg you . . . to give him your bodies, as a living sacrifice" (Phillips). Oh, we are to be consumed, then, but not destroyed! Life will still remain to us, but it will be God-controlled. What we will be doing is transferring responsibility, self-determination, from our own puny selves to the God who made us. And Paul says, this is a reasonable and sensible thing to do.

Even more is implied. This presentation is to be continuous as well as total. Many, in a moment of high commitment, have said with genuine abandonment and release, "Lord, take my life," but in the daily pressure have failed to preserve this lofty, shining ideal. Hands begin to perform their own tasks; feet to run their own errands; eyes, ears, mind, and will controlled at least in part by self. We find ourselves merely humming the tune when we should be singing it out, loud and clear,

> *All for Jesus! all for Jesus!*
> *All my being's ransomed pow'rs:*
> *All my tho'ts and words and doings,*
> *All my days and all my hours.*
>
> —MARY D. JAMES

We stand condemned. Misery accompanies incomplete consecration. There is no fulfillment—only doubts, struggles, remorse! And then in shame and self-reproach we renew our vows of total commitment and are warmed again by the assurance of acceptance and abandonment to Him. But what of those sagging times between commitments? What of the disastrous lapses in enthusiastic service? The beautiful transformation into the image of Christ which Paul promises is never made complete because of so many starts and stops.

Oh, friend, can we not learn that this must be a daily, an hourly saying and meaning, not only "Take my life," but

> *Take my MOMENTS and my DAYS,*
> *Let them flow in ceaseless praise.*

2

Take my MOMENTS and my DAYS, Let them flow in ceaseless praise.

And this makes the whole matter of consecration a completely different story. There is a moment of total giving over of self—a crisis experience. There must be. "All that I am, all that I ever shall be, is Thine!" But it is working out of the "shall be" that gives us trouble. The life we give must be reduced to days. The days must be reduced to moments, so that in every hour of every day the sacrifice of our lives is complete and constant.

Someone is thinking, "But I can't live under that sort of regimentation. I have to be free." Oh, my dear, that is where the beauty of it all lies, and the mystery! You see, you have given up your self-determination, your planning and programming, your calculating, your scheming, your presupposing, your obligation to "work things all out." You have given to God your life, your total self. But in doing so you have actually said, "You structure it for me daily. You make the itinerary; You draw the blueprint; You make the schedule; I have put myself in Your hands."

13

And this is not a dead, a passive thing. You don't go limp. You are to be a *living* sacrifice. The will of God is to be accomplished through the members of your body. The joy, the excitement, the verve, the challenge of doing are all there. The difference lies in the purpose, the motive, the ultimate objective. It is for *Him,* no longer for *self.*

The most precious endowment that God gave to the human race in creation was the right of choice, the power of self-determination. It distinguishes us from all His other creatures. This very power enables us to give ourselves back to Him. We can refuse to do so. We can yield or we can hold out. The noblest choice anyone can make is to say,

> *Take my MOMENTS and my DAYS,*
> *Let them flow in ceaseless praise.*

It is the moment that is important. It is not a whole conversation, but a single utterance that is significant. It is generally a moment that does the work. "Try him every moment," says the Scripture (Job 7:18). And when our moments are His, when that becomes a daily pattern of life, then truly we are a praise to God, for we have fulfilled His highest purpose in giving us the gift of life.

"Flow in ceaseless praise!" That does not mean we will be always singing a hymn or saying, "Glory to God!" Praise will be the tone, the color, the atmosphere of the flow of our moments.

The Rhone River rises from a glacier in the Swiss Alps. Glacial clay, picked up by the current as it flows, renders the water of the river almost opaque, brownish and dull. But during its course through Lake Geneva, it loses most of its clay. When it emerges it is clear blue and sparkling. Lord Byron described it as the "blue rushing of the arrowy Rhone." So our moments and our days, purged of the silt of self-centeredness, are colored with praise.

Ceaseless praise? Is this too much? How much does He deserve? He made you; He chose you; He loves you; He cares for you; He died for you!

Is *all* too much?

3

Take my HANDS, and let them move At the impulse of Thy love.

The hand is a marvelous organ of communication and is one of the most sensitive in the whole body. It reveals the inmost states of mind and feeling. It may corroborate or deny what the words are saying, but it is to be trusted. The open, outstretched palm speaks of acceptance and of giving and of blessing. The reversed palm speaks of rejection and denial. The closed hand speaks of resolve and determination. The clenched fist portrays intensity, even indignation. The index finger designates and makes personal. The trembling hand indicates weakness, insecurity, or strong emotion. The hand is capable of striking or of caressing, of lifting or of lying idle.

The hand carries out the bidding of the mind—stir the soup; put the key in the lock; write the letter; open the drawer; take the money; squeeze the throat.

Think of the structure of the hand: the palm with its cushioned strength, its firm grip; the fingers with their mobility, their independence, their skill. Contemplate the capability of the hand for evil. It is the hand that holds the gun, or the knife, or the needle. It is the fingerprint that identifies the criminal. But it is also the greatest instrument of service and blessing. It is the hand that writes the poem or performs the symphony; it is the hand that builds the temple or constructs the house; it is the hand that prepares the meals and keeps the home tidy and neat. It is the hand that reaches out to touch the lonely or the needy, that sends the dinner in to the bereaved family or picks the bouquet of flowers or dials the telephone number. It is the hand with which we take an oath. It is the hand that is given in marriage. It is the hand with which we salute the flag.

Think of the powerful descriptions of the hand as recorded in Scripture. Jesus said, "The hand of him that betrayeth me is with me on the table" (Luke 22:21). It was the hand that received the 30 pieces of silver, the price of our Lord's life. Hands drove the spikes that nailed Him to the Cross. Hands raised the instrument of torture and let it fall into its socket. Hands held the spear that was thrust into His side.

A moving story is told in Exod. 17:8-16. Israel was at war with Amalek and while Joshua fought with the enemy in the valley, Moses, Aaron, and Hur went up to the top of an adjoining hill. When Moses held up his hand, Israel prevailed, and when he let down his hand, Amalek prevailed.

But Moses' hands became weary. So he sat down upon a boulder and Aaron and Hur held up his hands, one on either side, and steadied his hands till the sun went down. So Israel was victor in the battle.

Laymen, have you ever used your hands to hold up the hands of your leader when he became weary and faint in the battle for righteousness and truth?

The Word charges us to "Be ye strong therefore, and let not your hands be weak: for your work shall be re-

17

warded" (2 Chron. 15:7). And the Psalmist sang, "Establish thou the work of our hands upon us; yea, the work of our hands establish thou it" (Ps. 90:17).

A number of years ago, Mrs. Sydney Martin of Glasgow, Scotland, told me of their experience when her husband left the coal mines to answer God's call to the ministry. Their apartment was in the back rooms of the church. The salary was £2.10 a week (about $10.00). World War II was just over and mere existence was a struggle.

I broke into the conversation to exclaim, "I don't know how you made it."

I shall never forget her reply. It was epic.

"Of course we made it," she said. *"I had these,"* and she held out her two beautiful, work-worn hands.

"Why," she said, "I bought yarn and I knitted socks and sweaters for little children. I bought material and made dresses for little girls and shirts for little boys and sold them. *Of course we made it! I had these!"*

God said to Moses, "What is that in thine hand?" It was a shepherd's staff. God used it to perform miracles.

For our hands to be really made ready for God's service, they must first be emptied.

> *My hands were filled with many things*
> *Which I did precious hold*
> *As any treasure of a king's*
> *Silver or gems or gold.*
> *The Master came and touched my hands*
> *The scars were on His own,*
> *And at His feet my treasures sweet,*
> *Fell shattered, one by one:*
> *"I must have empty hands," said He,*
> *"Wherewith to work My works through thee."*
> —Selected

18

Hands, to be used, must first be emptied. We can do this voluntarily, or God may bring an experience into our lives that itself empties our hands of the things we were holding too tightly—material values, a position, a dear one.

Look at your own hands! They may be wrinkled and misshapen with age or arthritis. They may be rough and strong with labor, or soft and fair with youth.

Have you ever actually said to God, "Here are my two hands. Take them! Use them! Let them be impelled by Thy love to all their tasks—homely, routine, arduous, even unpleasant." Love is the impulse for every duty when our hands are *His*. This does not mean that everything your hands shall do will be a religious act. It does mean that everything our hands do is done for *Him*.

Even as a teacher trains the hands of a musician, a typist, an artist with canvas, so He can teach our hands to become more skillful, more gentle. When you sit down to write that letter or card, ask God to guide your pen. What a ministry lies in the written word! Following my husband's death, I and my family received over 400 written communications. They were filled with very meaningful and beautiful words. I cannot estimate the comfort and support they gave me. God bless the hands that wrote those messages! I have prayed it again and again. They made God real to me. In my loneliness and my weariness, I seemed some days to have lost my direct touch with Him. He reached me by satellite and His message for me bounced off the pens of His children. I shall be eternally grateful.

It is the hands that reach out and touch. Therapists are recognizing the power of touch in caring for the newborn, the aged, the lonely, the mentally distressed or ill, the underprivileged, the eccentric.

19

Reach out and touch the heart of someone,
  Someone who's lost his way;
Helping him find a new direction,
  Showing him how to pray.

Reach out your hand to touch your neighbor,
  Even in little things;
Showing him inter'st in successes,
  Helping him with his needs.

Reach out your hand to help a stranger,
  Someone you've never known,
Someone who needs a friend to be close to,
  Someone who's all alone.

Reach out to those who are afflicted,
  Proving you really care;
Letting your love spill out in kindness,
  Willing to always share.

Reach out your hand to those who hate you,
  Letting them see your love;
Walking that extra mile with someone.
  Reach out your hand of love. *

—OTIS SKILLINGS

The handshake is a true revealer of personality. In 2 Kings 10:15 are these telling words, "Is thine heart right, as my heart is with thy heart? . . . If it be, give me thine hand." Especially among Christians, the handshake is a symbol of true relationship. Think of your own handshake. Is it weak and fishy? On the other hand, is it so gripping as to mutilate the receiver? Let it be firm yet gentle, warm yet reserved. It is more than a clasping of hands. It is an acceptance from the heart.

The touch of a hand can leave a permanent impression. I can still feel the hands of our godly pastor, Brother Ginn, laid on my eight-year-old head as he baptized me and prayed, "God, use this little girl to Thy glory. Set her apart this day to Thy service."

Sainted Martha Curry of New England laid her hands in blessing upon the head of our six-month-old baby boy, John. When God called him into the ministry 30 years later, I felt that her prayer had been answered.

I laid my hand on the shoulder of a discouraged Nazarene Bible College student one day as he sat dejectedly in class. He visibly responded. When class was over, he whispered as he passed by me, "Thank you for what you said to me." I hadn't uttered a word.

Tender hands, touching and healing, lifting and leading with gentle care. Strong hands upholding and defending, open hands giving good things, faithful hands, restraining and sustaining. Powerful hands building and supporting.

Take my HANDS, and let them move
At the impulse of Thy love.

4

Take my FEET, and let them be Swift and beautiful for Thee.

Isaiah said, "How beautiful upon the mountains are the feet of him that bringeth good tidings, that publisheth peace" (Isa. 52:7).

Feet that God controls are beautiful even if bare or cased in muddy boots. They may be in sandals or tennis shoes. They may wear Florsheims or Aigners or Red Cross Comforts. They may be shapely and vigorous or broken down and painful with overuse. But if they have been dedicated to Him, they are "swift and beautiful."

The last 15 months of my husband's life he was practically immobile. I did his walking for him; not just going to the store or watering the lawn, but moving to the bathroom counter to get the equipment to brush his teeth, or bringing the tray of food from the kitchen to his chair or bedside to serve him his meals. I literally took multiplied hundreds of steps for him. But I didn't begrudge one step. They were motivated by love.

He one day said, "You are beautiful, from the crown of your head to the soles of your feet." And I looked down at my poor old Number Nines encased in their comfortable, lumbering houseshoes, and I thought, Beautiful? Oh, guy! You're slipping!

But he was right. They were beautiful to him because they were serving him. And our feet will appear beautiful to the Lover of our souls if He recognizes that they have become weary and aching and calloused in service for Him.

Scripture has much to say about the feet and their use. We are told it is possible to run and not be weary; to walk and not faint (Isa. 40:31). Psalm 18:33 declares, "He maketh my feet like hinds' feet, and setteth me upon my high places."

Second Sam. 22:30 says, "By thee have I run through a troop: by my God have I leaped over a wall." Mic. 6:8 enjoins us, "Walk humbly with thy God." Col. 1:10 reminds us to "walk worthy" of the Lord; 1 Thess. 4:12 to "walk honestly"; Ps. 84:11 to "walk uprightly"; while in Gen. 17:1 God says, "Walk before me, and be thou perfect." Our walk, then, is our way of life.

But the feet were not only given us for locomotion. Sometimes the strongest position we can take is to *stand*. Stand firm! It takes yielded feet to do so. Some run because they are cowardly. Some walk away when they need to "stay put."

In Exod. 14:13, Moses said to the people, "Fear ye not, stand still, and see the salvation of the Lord."

First Cor. 16:13 urges us to "stand fast in the faith," and Eph. 6:13 commands us that having put on the armour of righteousness, and having done all *to* stand, we are to *stand* therefore!

Ps. 40:2 assures us, "He . . . set my feet upon a rock."

Standing glorifies God.

There is still another dimension to this matter of the dedicated feet. Josh. 14:9 says, "Surely the land whereon thy feet have trodden shall be thine inheritance, and thy children's for ever, because thou hast wholly followed the

Lord." And Josh. 1:3 adds, "Every place that the sole of your foot shall tread upon, that have I given unto you."

The territory we have taken in this battle for right and righteousness is not to be surrendered to the enemy. How much land once possessed by God's people in a spiritual sense has now been lost and is in the hands of the enemy! Responsibility for this rests not only with leadership but with the laity. I know that the character of a given area may change as years come and go. It is not mere physical location that is involved. But achievements for God should not be abandoned. It is a mistake to believe that change is always advancement. Jer. 6:16 gives us the word of God himself: "Stand ye in the ways, and see, and ask for the old paths, where is the good way, and walk therein, and ye shall find rest for your souls." A way is not necessarily good just because it is old. But that could be the very reason it *is* good! It has been tried. It has worked successfully. Hold your ground.

Yes, the feet are tremendously important in this matter of total involvement.

> *I read in a Book*
> *Of a Man*
> *Who "went about doing good."*
>
> *I wonder*
> *Why we are so well content*
> *With simply "going about."*

Covering a lot of territory, but really getting nowhere!

> *Take my FEET, and let them be*
> *Swift and beautiful for Thee.*

5

Take my VOICE, and let me sing
Always, only, for my King.

Singing, an important factor in Christian worship, is wide open to laymen. It was an outstanding feature of the worship of ancient Israel. At the height of Solomon's glory on celebration days, choirs were massed on the hills surrounding the Temple area. They sang antiphonally to the accompaniment of the cornet, the harp, the flute, the dulcimer, the organ, the cymbals, and the high sounding cymbals. Many of the psalms were thus sung to music. Can you not hear the majestic outpouring of sound as they rendered the following, Psalm 24? The choir arrangements are my own, but I can believe David had the same idea.

Choirs   The earth is the Lord's and the fulness thereof;
I and II   The world, and they that dwell therein.
           For he hath founded it upon the seas,
           And established it upon the floods.

Choir I   Who shall ascend into the hill of the Lord?
           Or who shall stand in his holy place?

Choir II	He that hath clean hands, and a pure heart;
	Who hath not lifted up his soul unto vanity,
	Nor sworn deceitfully.
	He shall receive the blessing from the Lord,
	And righteousness from the God of his salvation.
Choir I	Lift up your heads, O ye gates,
	And be ye lift up, ye everlasting doors;
	And the King of glory shall come in.
Choir II	Who is this King of glory?
Choir I	The Lord strong and mighty,
	The Lord mighty in battle.
Choir II	Lift up your heads, O ye gates;
	Even lift them up, ye everlasting doors,
	And the King of glory shall come in.
Choir I	Who is this King of glory?
Choirs I and II	The Lord of hosts, he is the King of glory.

The mechanism of the human organism that enables one to produce singing tones is intricate and delicate and wonderful. To some, more than others, this gift has been given. No director, however, should neglect the value and importance of congregational singing. Untrained, even ordinary voices, if singing in tune and in harmony, can make a joyful noise unto the Lord. There is something contagious and uplifting in hearing a congregation of lay men and women lift their voices in jubilant song. It has a unifying effect upon all the features of the service which follow. Psalm 100:2 urges us to "Come before his presence with singing." When sung in the Spirit and with the understanding, the result is profound.

Congregations should be encouraged to sing thoughtfully, noting the message of the words being sung. It is easy to fall into the habit of following a familiar melody with the mind wandering and the soul unresponding. Scolding will do little good to improve the situation. Pausing to read the words aloud will sometimes quicken realization. Our forefathers used to "line" the hymns for this very purpose. Having a verse sung solo will often produce a salutary result. Sometimes the interjection of a related experience will deepen realization of the words of the song. Prayerful preparation on the part of the leader for directing the singing will produce amazing results.

Choirs, too, are a valuable medium for laypeople to participate in and exercise God-given talents. Trained by knowledgeable persons, they add effectively to the celebration of special events in the church calendar as well as to the regular services. They set the tone and the mood for the preacher.

Relatively few have outstanding gifts for singing. These have no doubt been recognized and have received a special musical education. Sometimes it is the joy of a religious leader to discover a diamond in the rough and bring that one into recognition within the fold of the church.

And now a word of warning. Perhaps nowhere in all the couplets of Frances Havergal's noble hymn is there more danger than at this point. The musical program of the church has been nicknamed by some wag "the war department." Anyone who has a voice to sing should daily pray,

> Take my VOICE, and let me sing
> Always, only, for my King.

Perhaps because music can produce such a spectacular impression, singers are particularly vulnerable to the sin of pride. Following a performance, one becomes the recipient of compliment and praise. This is right and a proper means of encouragement. But it can become a snare. The singer must immediately turn that praise back to the One who bestowed the gift of a singing voice and humbly receive it only in His name.

Furthermore, there is the peculiar temptation to jealousy and competition among singers. Hidden resentments can corrode the spirit and destroy the beauty of any presentation.

"I don't know why she always gets the solo parts. She can't sing for sour apples."

"He has sung a special three Sundays in a row! He's not all that good!"

Too, singers can become opinionated, rigid about where they will sing and what they will sing, about who will and who won't like it, and about what will "go over."

In choosing a number for a special, one is always safe in singing the Word of God. It is quick and powerful. And one is assured of acceptance, for God has said, "My Word . . . shall not return unto me void, but it shall accomplish that which I please, and it shall prosper in the thing whereto I sent it" (Isa. 55:11). Psalms 27, 23, 24, and Isaiah 55 have all been set to music and hundreds of other songs and hymns derive their language directly from the Word.

One area in which lay men and women can render effective service is in training children and youth to sing. You will be captivating the parents' as well as the children's interests, for they will be proud to hear their youngsters perform. You need not be a solo singer yourself to excel in this area. But your enthusiastic training of the children and youth will be most rewarding. Let your expectations go high. Children will memorize words and music. Require it of them. They will try harmonizing. Train their ears to sing in tune. They will respond to shading, to interpretation, to the legatos and the crescendos that make their effort a real production. And they will love public appearances. Costume them in some appropriate robes and you will be thus controlling the touchy subject of dress for both boys and girls. To become their director, you should know something about music and good diction, but you don't need to sport a pink tassel on your mortar board or have either a Bachelor of Music or a Master of Music degree.

Music publishers are producing a variety of numbers of varying levels of difficulty. You can use either live or recorded accompaniment, so even the smaller churches, of which there are vastly more than there are larger ones, can initiate this program.

In this, as in all the areas examined whether one be performing solo or in a group great or small, the motive must be for His sake and in His name.

> *Take my VOICE, and let me sing*
> *Always, only, for my King.*

It will take constant heart-searching to keep it so.

6

Take my LIPS, and let them be Filled with messages for Thee.

Oh, the power of language and of the speaking voice!
In spite of the marvelous advances in the various mediums
of communication, the spoken word is still the most
effective of them all.

We are thinking now not of the prepared speech or
message such as the minister might give for a designated
service or occasion. We are talking about the spontaneous
conversation that goes on in families, at social events, in
casual encounters, over the telephone, wherever two or
more people communicate. "Lord, 'Take my lips' at these
times, not only when I stand to testify or bear my witness."

Reduced to its most elemental form, this whole matter
of speaking is simply first, what we say; and second, the
way we say it. Christians should ever be busy filling their
reservoirs with worthwhile subjects and ideas to talk
about. This is accomplished through reading, through lis-
tening, through observation and association of ideas,
through stimulation of memory, and through meditation.
Meditation—almost a lost art! "While I was musing the
fire burned," said the Psalmist (Ps. 39:3). If we are

thinking upon noble, uplifting, worthwhile, interesting, and expansive subjects when we are alone or in our silences, we will find we have something appropriate to say in every conversation.

And the way we say it! The study of language is a lifetime task. And what an enjoyable one! There are apt, acceptable, telling, powerful words that are to be found in our reading vocabularies but are seldom heard in our oral ones. Cultivate skill in expressing yourself. And even more than language, the spirit in which we clothe our words is vital. We can be confident without being aggressive; convincing without being dictatorial; pleasant without being effusive; warm without being flattering. Harsh, biting, sarcastic, taunting, cruel words have no place on the lips of a Christian.

The art of conversation needs to be cultivated. This means you will strive to be a good listener—to your five-year-old, your teenager, your spouse, your neighbor, your fellow board member. Listen with an open mind. Try to get the other person's point of view without marshalling a silent rebuttal to everything he says. Try to understand him even if you do not agree with him. Don't shut him off!

To be a good conversationalist, you will seek to find common ground. Determine the areas of agreement, of interest, of concern. Guard against monopolizing the time. Stimulate interchange. Seek to lift the tone of the conversation. Don't be afraid to introduce a spiritual thought. Your interlocutor may be expecting you to do so and may be disappointed if you don't.

The spoken word is capable of
informing or deceiving,
instructing or discouraging,
comforting or defeating,
uplifting or degrading.

"Set a watch, O Lord, before my mouth; keep the door of my lips" (Ps. 141:3).

If we are sensitive, the inner voice will warn us when we are about to repeat a tale or give out some information or pronounce a judgment that is not truly a "message from God." We have all had this happen. A very candid, down-to-earth friend of mine confessed for us all. She said, "I start sometimes to say something and God reminds me not to do it, but I want so much to say it, I go ahead. Then I have to ask God, and sometimes the people, to forgive me."

"The tongue is a fire, a world of iniquity: so is the tongue among our members, that it defileth the whole body, and setteth on fire the course of nature; and it is set on fire of hell" (Jas. 3:6).

"Keep thy tongue from evil, and thy lips from speaking guile" (Ps. 34:13).

"There is . . . a time to speak," says the Wise Man (Eccles. 3:7, NIV). And there will be occasions when we as laymen have golden opportunities "to speak the word in season." One occasion is when death has come into a home. The minister is expected to have words of comfort and assurance ready. But how beautiful if laymen and laywomen, too, can bring a message direct from God. Nothing is so applicable as His Word. Memorize suitable words of blessing and quote them upon such occasions.

A number of years ago the daughter of one of my husband's colleagues suffered the tragic and unexpected loss of her young husband. We called in the home along with many friends to offer our condolences. My husband's word to the stricken wife was, "The God of all grace, who hath called us unto his eternal glory by Christ Jesus, after that ye have suffered a while, make you perfect, stablish, strengthen, settle you. To him be glory and dominion for ever and ever. Amen" (1 Pet. 5:10-11).

That was all. The following morning we had not left the breakfast table when the phone rang. It was my husband's colleague. He said, "Yesterday some words were spoken to our daughter. Among the scores of things that were said, it is the only thing she remembers. It was something about 'after that you have suffered a while, make you perfect.' She cannot recall who said those words. I thought it sounded like you. G. B., where is that reference?"

Nothing is so meaningful as the Word of God.

Another opportunity for effective speech is in public prayer. Practice aloud in private, and your public prayers will be charged with meaning and with power. If you know beforehand that you will be called upon to pray in public, give some careful preparation to the probable content and delivery of your prayer. It was Jesus who gave us the model prayer. Prayer to be spontaneous need not be impromptu.

As in all else, the Master is our Example. Grace and truth poured from His lips. An infinite wealth of tenderness and wisdom characterized His speech. Whether teaching, warning, counseling, or comforting, His words were controlled by the Father. Certainly, "never man spake like this man." If His love fills our hearts and motivates every utterance, the words we speak will be like messages from Him. This should not be the exception, but the rule.

> *Be like Jesus, this my song,*
> *In the home and in the throng;*
> *Be like Jesus, all day long!*
> *I would be like Jesus.* *

> *Take my LIPS, and let them be*
> *Filled with messages for Thee.*

7

Take my SILVER and my GOLD;
Not a mite would I withhold.

The opportunity to give of our material means and the inclination to do so are natural consequences of a life totally committed to God.

How refreshing it would be if we could have a widespread repeat of the circumstances recorded in Exodus, Chapters 35 and 36. The children of Israel had been challenged by their leader, Moses, to bring in of their material possessions to build the tabernacle. And they responded. The Scriptures say, "Everyone who was willing and whose heart moved him came and brought an offering to the Lord . . . All who were willing . . . came" (Exod. 35:21-22, NIV). Each one brought what he had—gold, silver, brass, jewelry, precious stones, acacia wood. The women spun articles of blue, purple, scarlet, and fine linen, and they brought freewill offerings every morning. At last those in charge said to Moses, "You're going to have to tell the people not to bring any more. We have all we can possibly use and too much!"

Imagine it! If that should happen in your church next Sunday, if your pastor has to tell the people to stop giving, please let me know about it.

What were the causes of this abundant response? First, obedience; obedience not only to their leader and his appeal, but obedience to God who prompted them to this sacrificial display. Second, love; love for God and for the advancement of His kingdom. Love and gratitude to Him who had given them the gifts they were now in part returning to Him. There was enthusiasm, too, and a sense of righteous pride that the work of God should not fall into disrepute.

Awareness of Christ's sacrificial death for us should ever move us to liberality—"Though he was rich, yet for your sakes he became poor, that ye through his poverty might be rich" (2 Cor. 8:9). He emptied himself. He considered that equality with God was not something to be grasped, but He took upon Him the form of a servant and became subject unto death, even the death of the cross.

Awareness, too, of human need should move us to a compassionate response. John says, "If anyone has material possessions and sees his brother in need but has no pity on him, how can the love of God be in him?" (1 John 3:17, NIV). Not only can we assist those in need with money, but with articles of clothing and household effects which we are no longer using. Accumulations of such things add to the clutter of our homes and prevent their utilization by those who are actually in want.

The Bible has set the proportionate level of our giving, "As God has prospered you" (1 Cor. 16:2). There is no record of either giving "much" or "little" in God's books. "If there be first a willing mind, it is accepted according to that a man hath and not according to that he hath not" (2 Cor. 8:12). The willingness must be accompanied by a performance. How many of us in a moment of high resolve when the appeal came strong and clear have made the silent promise to ourselves, I will respond; I will give.

But the moment passes, the vision fades, the commitment is never made and we dismiss the nagging reminders with the thought, It was just an impulse. We need not be unrealistic, but we should trust the generous impressions that come in hours of high revelation and special insight, and act upon them.

The Scriptures tell us that God owns all the silver and gold in the earth. The cattle upon a thousand hills are His. He loans man His resources for use and for development. But it is only on loan. Some, through inheritance or skillful investment or hard work, have accumulated more of this world's goods than others. This is not occasion for pride on their part nor for jealousy on the part of their fellow Christians. We are workers together. The amount of our contribution is not the measure of our liberality. God looks on the heart. He knows what we have *not* as well as what we have. He knows our fixed income, our medical emergency, the number of our dependents. He knows whether we are telling the truth when we say,

"Not a mite would I withhold."

A beautiful story is recorded in 2 Samuel 24. David the king had counted the people in disobedience to God's command and as a consequence God had sent a plague that was destroying the people of Israel. In repentance, David desired to build an altar and make a sacrifice to God that the plague might be stayed. He sought to buy the parcel of ground where Araunah, the Jebusite, had a threshing floor as a place upon which to erect the altar.

Araunah learned of David's desire to purchase the land and offered to give it as a gift to the king. David's reply was sublime. "No," he said, "I insist on paying you for it. I will not sacrifice to the Lord my God . . . offerings that cost me nothing" (2 Sam. 24:24, NIV).

What a slogan for Christian laymen to adopt! He gave

36

His all that we might be saved. In comparison, our little store of silver and gold is so meager. Must we be grudging in its distribution? There is "that scattereth and yet increaseth; and there is that withholdeth more than is meet, but it tendeth to poverty" (Prov. 11:24). Can we not say from our hearts,

> *Take my SILVER and my GOLD;*
> *Not a mite would I withhold.*

8

Take my INTELLECT, and use
Every power as Thou shalt choose.

Amazing is the capability and the versatility of the human mind. Certainly few, if any, have exhausted its possibilities. And the tragedy is that all too many actually stop using and developing their intellects long before old age comes upon them.

Think of the vast resources of the mind in the areas of reasoning, of judgment, of memory, of imagination, of creativity, of insight, of comprehension, of philosophy. The mind is capable of ascending to sublime heights of contemplation. Conceive of these faculties all dedicated to God, all used by Him in His service! Think of one individual so committed! Think of a thousand! It is a staggering thought.

Some have or think they have less than the average share of intellect. This gives them excuse to not make the most of what they do have. They use only as much mental power as they must to get by. They are like the one-talent man who hid his gift in the earth and failed to invest it in worthwhile endeavor. He was a disappointment to the Master and He received a stern rebuke.

There are others who think they have rather more than the average allotment of brain power. Their danger is twofold. They may become proud and opinionated and thus alienate themselves from the very ones who need their superior abilities. Intellectual pride is the most obnoxious kind of pride. Or they may isolate themselves from others under the delusion that no one really has the ability to comprehend and appreciate their greatness. Alone in their ivory towers, they are at the service of neither God nor man. We all must realize that whatever God has given, and all that He has given, He will use if we will allow Him to do so.

Every intellect needs to be challenged. We tend to respond to demand. This is the magnificent opportunity for lay men and women. Unbelievable potential is locked up in the minds of ordinary people. Leadership everywhere needs to realize that the sharing of responsibility will produce far richer results than attempting to carry it all alone.

This fact is graphically described in Exod. 18:12-27. Moses, Israel's great leader, was bearing the burden alone and was taking himself far too seriously. He received a visit from Jethro, his father-in-law. (Now, hearken! Inlaws are good for something!) Moses' father-in-law observed him all of one day from morning until evening as he judged every matter, great or small, that the people brought to him. By nightfall Moses was worn out, but he explained that he was instructing the people in the ways of the Lord and that what he was doing was very important.

His father-in-law replied, "But it's no good! You're going to have a nervous breakdown." (The King James Version has it "wear away." It means the same thing.) And Jethro said, "You need help!"

Then he gave Moses a workable plan. He told him to choose from among the people "able men" (those with

39

sharp minds), God-fearing men, men of integrity, and make them counselors—for groups of 1,000, of 100, of 50, and of 10 according to their several abilities. All minor matters were to be brought to them for judgment. Moses was still to handle the major problems.

Moses saw the reasonableness of the idea and adopted it. And it worked! Moses' strength was conserved and think of all those laymen who got a job to do! How much better than for one leader to be trying to do it all. (I should be talking to pastors. But hopefully the word will get out.)

In the list of inspiring and descriptive names given to the Son of God as found in Isa. 9:6, *Counsellor* appears at the head of the list. "His name shall be called Wonderful, Counsellor, The mighty God, The everlasting Father, The Prince of Peace." This title signifies that to all who say "Take my intellect," He will impart the sagacity, the good judgment, the discernment, the ability to perform any task assigned. He will be your Counsellor. There are resources available from which we can gain knowledge and skill to successfully carry out every program for which we are responsible. The mind likes to be used, it likes to be trusted. And there is an exhilaration that comes from mental accomplishment that even transcends the rewards for physical endeavor.

The mind has tremendous power over the physical body. As a man thinketh in his heart, so is he. Control of the body depends in large part upon the thought life. Phil. 4:8 enjoins us, "Whatsoever things are true, whatsoever things are honest, whatsoever things are just, whatsoever things are pure, whatsoever things are lovely, whatsoever things are of good report; if there be any virtue, and if there be any praise, think of these things." Directing the mind to dwell upon good, true, beautiful, praiseworthy subjects affects the health, the entire personality of the individual. In like manner, to cherish mean, ugly, suspicious, unworthy, jealous thoughts subtly undermines the whole character.

In times of distress and perplexity, of loneliness and uncertainty, Isa. 26:3 declares, "Thou wilt keep him in perfect peace, whose mind is stayed on thee." Fixing the entire attention deliberately, voluntarily on the Lord drives from the attention thoughts of evil which the enemy seeks to insinuate.

A positive mental attitude is the antidote for fear and despondency. 2 Tim. 1:7 declares, "God hath not given us the spirit of fear; but of power, and of love, and of a sound mind." (The NIV has it "self-discipline.") Perhaps nowhere do we need to exercise control as in the use of the mind. When we totally turn our minds over to the Spirit of God, we are actually putting Him in the pilot's seat. Self-indulgence at this point becomes sin to us. No one else may know what is going on in our minds, but God knows and reads our thoughts as though they were an open book. Only the power of God working in us will enable us to think God's thoughts after Him. "The Lord searcheth all hearts, and understandeth all the imaginations of the thoughts: if thou seek him, he will be found of thee" (1 Chron. 28:9).

We need to pray, "Search me, O God, and know my heart: try me, and know my thoughts: and see if there be any wicked way in me, and lead me in the way everlasting" (Ps. 139:23-24). Failure to control the thought life can lead to dismal breakdowns—moral, emotional, marital, social, spiritual. It need not be so if we have said and truly meant,

> *Take my INTELLECT, and use*
> *Every power as Thou shalt choose.*

The most beautiful character quality that can accompany a brilliant mind is humility. Dr. Chapman drew a lovely analogy from a field of ripened grain when he said, "Full heads bow down!" All we have we have

41

received from Him. "In whom are hid all the treasures of wisdom and knowledge" (Col. 2:3). May Paul's prayer for the Colossian Christians find an echo in our own prayer life: "That ye might be filled with the knowledge of his will in all wisdom and spiritual understanding; That ye might walk worthy of the Lord unto all pleasing, being fruitful in every good work, and increasing in the knowledge of God" (Col. 1:9-10).

9

Take my WILL and make it Thine;
It shall be no longer mine.

Take my will! It is easier to say, take my hands, take my feet, take my voice. And it is more temporary. We use them only on occasion. There is a finality about saying, "Take my will." This represents a constant state of mind, a maintained attitude of surrender, of yielding, of resignation, of giving up. It strikes at the very core of our beings. The right to say no is a cherished right. We began exercising it early in life. The effectiveness of our first attempt at self-assertion probably was determined by the kind of home we were reared in. I recall that the first time I tried it I got to stand in the corner with my face to the wall. I learned through bitter experience not to verbalize my will, but the no was there and the right to it, I prized.

But Tennyson has said,

> *Our wills are ours, we know not how.*
> *Our wills are ours, to make them Thine!*
> *—In Memoriam*

Ah! That is the crux of the matter. God has endowed us with this superlative gift, a will of our own. But His

43

purpose in giving us this faculty was that we might voluntarily say, "Lord, it is Thine."

> *Not what I wish to be,*
> *Nor where I wish to go,*
> *For who am I that I should choose my way?*
> *The Lord shall choose for me;*
> *'Tis better far, I know.*
> *So let Him bid me go, or stay.**

—C. AUSTIN MILES

I shall never forget the Treble Tone Trio—Garvin, Collins, and Dunbar—singing those words in an Olivet College chapel service many years ago. Thank you, ladies! It has been the theme song of my life. "The Lord shall choose for me." Some of His choices down through the years have been painful and mysterious, but I maintain that they have been *right* and *"better far."*

Why is it so hard to say, "Take my will?" Why is it so hard to maintain that attitude?

First, probably it is because of fear. Fear of the unknown. Fear of just what this surrender involves. We do not understand, sometimes we have not been told, that in giving Him our wills, they are not to be broken, or even bent. They are to be blended with His will—His all-seeing, all-knowing will. Our horizons are so circumscribed. We see only the realities of this little life and we sometimes have a false concept of God the Father. He is not trying to force us into doing something that is wholly distasteful to us or for which we are by nature unprepared. He has made us. His will is on our side. He knows our potential. He wants to bring us to the point of greatest fulfillment, of supreme joy and happiness, not only for this brief span of years we are to spend on earth, but for all eternity.

God is not a sadist. He does not delight in our subjugation. He has plans for us that cannot be revealed or realized until we have said with total abandonment, "Take my will."

Another reason why we hesitate to make this commitment is a lack of faith. We want to read the last chapter in the book and make sure it's going to come out all right before we buy the book. But this walk with God is a walk of faith, not of sight. When we fail to trust Him with our future, we grieve the great Father-heart of God. We are not only discounting His ability to lead and guide us, we are actually saying by implication, "I can plan my life better than You can. I am more sure of myself than I am of You. I have my best interests at heart more than You do." Doubt and mistrust can paralyze the will and make it incapable of acting positively.

A further reason why we stop short of saying, "Thy will be done," is a lack of love—a lack in the measure of our love for God on the one hand, and a lack of understanding His great love for us on the other. Deep love for any object makes us want to give ourselves unreservedly to it. It may be the love of knowledge. The hours spent in reading and study are never begrudged by the true student. Love prompts the action. The scientist, the musician, the artist spend uncounted hours in their laboratories and studios perfecting the skills of their chosen professions. Outpoured love for a child or a life partner is unmeasured in times of illness or anxiety or stress. Love is uncalculating. Love cannot do enough. If we are experiencing difficulty in saying, "Take my will, O make it Thine," we need to pray for a baptism of love. This often comes by contemplation of God's great love for us, manifested in our creation and in the provisions for our redemption. Consider the gift of God's Son, His life on earth, His sacrificial death, His mediatorial pleading for us even now.

Forbid it, Lord, that I should boast,
  Save in the death of Christ, my God.
All the vain things that charm me most,
  I sacrifice them to His blood.

See, from His head, His hands, His feet,
  Sorrow and love flow mingled down,
Did e'er such love and sorrow meet,
  Or thorns compose so rich a crown?

Were the whole realm of nature mine,
  That were a present far too small.
Love so amazing, so divine,
  Demands my soul, my life, my all.
                    —Isaac Watts

Jesus is our supreme Example. His will was totally blended with that of His Father. He prayed in the Garden of Gethsemane, "O my Father, if it be possible, let this cup pass from me: nevertheless not as I will, but as thou wilt" (Matt. 26:39). How many of us pray, "Let this cup pass" and fail to say the "nevertheless"—"nevertheless, not my will but Thine be done." Jesus said He came "to do the will of him that sent me" (John 4:34), and again in John 5:30 He repeated, "I seek not mine own will."

Nay, but I yield, I yield;
  I can hold out no more.
I sink, by dying love compelled,
  And own Thee, Conqueror.
                    —Charles Wesley

Sometimes on the complicated journey of life we are perplexed as to just what the will of God for us in a given situation is. Patient waiting before God will show us the way. "He that believeth shall not make haste," says Isa.

28:16, and again, "If any man will do his will, he shall know" (John 7:17). Eph. 5:17 speaks of "understanding what the will of the Lord is."

If we keep our commitment inviolate, God will vindicate His promise to guide us continually. He has said, "The meek will he guide in judgment" (Ps. 25:9). In Ps. 32:8 He assures us, "I will guide thee with mine eye," and Ps. 48:14 promises, "He will be our guide even unto death."

Lord, I love You enough and I trust You enough to say,

Take my WILL and make it Thine;
It shall be no longer mine.

10

Take my HEART; it is Thine own!
It shall be Thy royal throne.

"Keep thy heart with all diligence; for out of it are the issues of life" (Prov. 4:23), says the Wise Man. The heart is the seat of the affections. It is the barometer which gauges emotional response. It is the source of our motivation. It, with the approval of the intellect, supplies purpose, drive, enthusiasm, stability. "Is your heart right?" is a pertinent question. "Follow your heart" is safe advice if the heart has been established in righteousness.

Scripture has many designations for the heart. On the one hand it is described as evil, desperately wicked, weak, deceitful, rebellious, hard, stony, proud, perverse, and foolish. But God can make the heart clean, good, honest, contrite, true, tender, pure, glad, and wise.

We say to one who is discouraged, "Take heart." We describe one in whom there is no milk of human kindness as being "heartless." We speak of a crushing grief as being "heartbreaking," and of anguish of the mind as "heartache," and of that which is deeply experienced as "heartfelt." The physical heart, the organ that pumps the blood that keeps our bodies alive and functioning, is absolutely necessary to existence. So this inner heart, the very center of our beings, is essential to our spiritual well-being and determines the effectiveness of our service to God. The heart is responsible for action. We need to say daily,

Take my HEART; it is Thine own!
It shall be Thy royal throne.

The Spirit of God must occupy the place of supreme and unrivaled authority in our hearts. If self or any other interest or person takes preeminence, then our entire commitment to God becomes jeopardized. How can the feet perform His bidding, or the hands move only at His impulse, or the voice speak only His message if He is not occupying the throne of the heart? He is either Lord of all or else He is not Lord at all!

The Word of God gives us some guidelines to follow in this matter. Ps. 57:7 declares, "My heart is fixed, O God, my heart is fixed: I will sing and give praise." It is possible to make one's convictions so firm and settled that the heart is fixed. There is no mental reservation, no provision to loose the moorings of the soul and drift. Allegiance to God is for now and forever. Determination has been made and the course set. We are told that Daniel "purposed in his heart that he would not defile himself with the portion of the king's meat" (Dan. 1:8). That settled it. There was no equivocation. He showed the same tenacity of fixed purpose when his enemies at court sought to secure his destruction by making the worship of his God a criminal offense. The den of lions did not dissuade him from opening his windows toward Jerusalem three times a day, praying to the God of Israel. There was no hesitation, no weighing of possible alternatives. His heart was fixed.

What a grievous disappointment it is to learn that one in whose life and experience we have trusted has fallen from the lofty estimation of friends and fellow churchmen. Usually the failure comes from a heart that was not established in holiness. Piles of slag thrown up near the coal mines of Wales by the miners themselves had been there so long the people of Aberfan thought they were the "everlasting hills," and built the schoolhouse at the base of one of them. One day the hill collapsed, burying alive the children of that entire village. Let us pray to God that we may be so rooted and grounded in Him that with Charles Wesley we can sing of a heart

> *Which neither life nor death can part*
> *From Him that dwells within.*

The natural consequence of the fixed heart is rejoicing. "O God, my heart is fixed: I will sing and give praise." In this world of change and uncertainty, of shifting moral values and of disastrous failures, it is cause for gladness that one can actually set his affections on things above, not on things on the earth. Then "when Christ, who is our life, shall appear," we shall also appear with Him in glory (Col. 3:4). This is security, security for all eternity. It is not automatic, but it is a day-by-day possibility.

A second quality of a heart made right is set forth in Ps. 112:7, "His heart is fixed, trusting in the Lord." A heart whose purpose is fixed has put its trust implicitly in God. This takes away the strain, the set jaw, the tight fist, the grim determination to hold on till the bitter end. The Lord has agreed to keep that which we have committed unto Him, and when we have deliberately set our course to be true to Him, trust comes easy.

Trust is assured reliance on the character, the ability, the strength, and the truth of God. The basis for our trust is His infallible Word. "Hath he said, and shall he not do

50

it? or hath he spoken, and shall he not make it good?" (Num. 23:19). Hear His unfailing promises! "The Lord redeemeth the soul of his servants: and none of them that trust in him shall be desolate" (Ps. 34:22).

"Trust ye in the Lord for ever; for in the Lord Jehovah is everlasting strength" (Isa. 26:4).

"The Lord is my rock, and my fortress, and my deliverer; my God, my strength, in whom I will trust" (Ps. 18:2).

"They that trust in the Lord shall be as mount Zion, which cannot be removed, but abideth for ever" (Ps. 125:1).

"My soul trusteth in thee: yea, in the shadow of thy wings will I make my refuge, until these calamities be overpast" (Ps. 57:1).

"Be strong and of good courage . . . fear not, nor be dismayed: for the Lord God, even my God, will be with thee; he will not fail thee" (1 Chron. 28:20).

William F. Lloyd has written,

> *My times are in Thy hand,*
> *My God, I wish them there;*
> *My life, my friends, my soul, I leave*
> *Entirely to Thy care.*

This is the trusting heart!

> *Then all is peace and light*
> *This soul within;*
> *Thus shall I walk with Thee,*
> *The Loved Unseen;*
> *Leaning on Thee, my God,*
> *Guided along the road,*
> *Nothing between.*
>
> —H. BONAR

Perfect trust!

There is a third quality of the heart that God inspires, and that is the *burning* heart. The two who walked with Jesus on the road to Emmaus following His resurrection said, "Did not our heart burn within us, while he talked with us by the way, and while he opened to us the scriptures?" (Luke 24:32). Our hearts will burn as we talk with Him and meditate upon His Word. It is written of John the Baptist that he was a burning and a shining light. At Pentecost flames of fire sat upon the heads of the apostles as a symbol of the burning baptism with the Holy Spirit which they received.

Fire in Scriptures is a symbol of destruction and of punishment. But it is also a symbol of illumination, of intensity, of purifying.

> *Refining fire, go through my heart,*
> *Illuminate my soul;*
> *Scatter thy life through every part,*
> *And sanctify the whole.*
>
> *O, that it now from heav'n might fall*
> *And all my sins consume!*
> *Come, Holy Ghost, on Thee I call;*
> *Spirit of burning, come!*
> —CHARLES WESLEY

I am hearing these days about something else—something called "burnout." I'm reading about it, especially in religious magazines. Lawyers, doctors, teachers, preachers are talking about it; a lagging in their enthusiasm for their profession; a desire to quit and give up; interest has sagged; the rewards are inadequate; there is a lack of fulfillment.

Now it must be recognized that physical and psychological factors may be involved. The body may have been pressured without proper time given to rest and relaxation. Competition and the strain to achieve may have sapped emotional energy until the spirit rebels. Failure on the part of others to respond or cooperate may have heightened one's disappointment and discouragement.

But in this matter of service to God, the real cause of the loss of interest and enthusiasm may actually be "heart failure"—a "heart attack"—"cardiac arrest," if you please! Our constant theme song must be,

> *A heart resigned, submissive, meek,*
> *My great Redeemer's throne,*
> *Where only Christ is heard to speak,*
> *Where Jesus reigns alone.*
> —CHARLES WESLEY

Jeremiah, the prophet, suffered symptoms of genuine "burnout" several times. It really isn't anything new! At one time, he even contemplated "getting away from it all" by buying up a motel out in the wilderness. (The King James Version calls it a lodge.) Here he could be free from the people who had refused to support him. Here he could deal only with strangers, transients whom he might see only over one night, or at the most for a weekend. He would get by with "witnessing" occasionally. It sounded like a capital idea (Jer. 9:2).

But he couldn't do it! He said God's Word was in his heart as a *burning fire,* shut up in his bones, and he could not quit (Jer. 20:9).

I guess it is a case of fighting fire with fire. When the enemy tells us we are experiencing "burnout," God's Holy Spirit can kindle a fire in our hearts so hot that we will be set aflame with holy zeal. We must provide the fuel through prayer and meditation on the Word. He provides the fire.

53

Oh, my dear friend, how is it with you? Are you experiencing a "burnout" or can you say,

> 'Tis burning in my soul,
> The fire of heavenly love is burning in my soul.
>
> —Delia White

If He is truly on the throne, then He will keep our hearts ablaze. Take your heart's temperature. If it's low, do something about it!

II

Take my LOVE; my God, I pour
At Thy feet its treasure store.

Love must find expression. If it doesn't, it dries up. The only love worth talking about is outpoured love.

We present-day disciples of the Lord need to relive the poignantly beautiful scene that transpired between Peter and Jesus that morning on the shores of Tiberias, following the Master's resurrection (John 21:15-17). When they had dined on the breakfast of fish and bread Jesus had prepared, He drew Peter aside and asked him the searching question, "Simon, son of Jonas, lovest thou me more than these?"

These what? Probably these boats, these nets, this fishing gear, all of these things pertaining to the life that absorbed Peter before he left them to follow Christ. "'These things' you returned to, Peter, when you had denied Me and were disheartened and disillusioned and ashamed. 'These things' which, unless you come to love Me *supremely,* will always draw you back to the life you once pursued."

Three times Jesus put the love test to Peter. Three times Peter protested, "I do love You." And three times

Jesus answered, "Prove it, then. Prove it by your outpoured love. 'Feed my lambs.' 'Feed my sheep.' That is how I will know that you love Me."

Love is not a protestation of affection. Love is action.

Everywhere people are crying out for a practical demonstration of love. An unknown author has put it bluntly:

> *I was hungry,*
> *and you formed a humanities*
> *club and discussed my hunger.*
> *Thank you.*
>
> *I was imprisoned,*
> *and you crept off quietly*
> *and prayed for my release.*
>
> *I was naked,*
> *and in your mind*
> *you debated the morality of*
> *my appearance.*
>
> *I was sick,*
> *and you knelt and thanked God*
> *for your health.*
>
> *I was homeless,*
> *and you preached to me*
> *of the spiritual shelter*
> *of the love of God.*
>
> *I was lonely,*
> *and you left me alone*
> *to pray for me.*

You seem so holy—
so close to God.
But I'm still very hungry
and lonely
and cold.

So where
have your prayers gone?
What does it profit a man
to page through
his book of prayers
when the rest of the world
is crying for his help?

Jesus' judgment is clearly pronounced upon those who in their lifetimes have not demonstrated love.

When the Son of man shall come in his glory, and all the holy angels with him, then shall he sit upon the throne of his glory: and before him shall be gathered all nations: and he shall separate them one from another, as a shepherd divideth his sheep from the goats: and he shall set the sheep on his right hand, but the goats on the left.

Then shall the King say unto them on his right hand, Come, ye blessed of my Father, inherit the kingdom prepared for you from the foundation of the world: For I was an hungred, and ye gave me meat: I was thirsty, and ye gave me drink: I was a stranger, and ye took me in: naked, and ye clothed me: I was sick, and ye visited me: I was in prison, and ye came unto me.

Then shall the righteous answer him, saying, Lord, when saw we thee an hungred, and fed thee? or thirsty, and gave thee drink? When saw we thee a stranger, and took thee in? or naked, and clothed thee? Or when saw we thee sick, or in prison, and came unto thee?

And the King shall answer and say unto them, Verily I say unto you, Inasmuch as ye have done it unto

57

one of the least of these my brethren, ye have done it unto me.

Then shall he say also unto them on the left hand, Depart from me, ye cursed, into everlasting fire, prepared for the devil and his angels: for I was an hungred, and ye gave me no meat: I was thirsty, and ye gave me no drink: I was a stranger, and ye took me not in: naked, and ye clothed me not: sick, and in prison, and ye visited me not.

Then shall they also answer him, saying, Lord when saw we thee an hungred, or athirst, or a stranger, or naked, or sick, or in prison, and did not minister unto thee?

Then shall he answer them, saying, Verily I say unto you, Inasmuch as ye did it not to one of the least of these, ye did it not to me.

And these shall go away into everlasting punishment: but the righteous into life eternal (Matt. 25:31-46).

We are to minister first to those of the household of faith, our brethren in the church and the fellowship. Then we are to reach out the helping hand to any who are in need; to the hungry, to the sick, to the lonely, to the imprisoned—imprisoned in body or in mind or in spirit.

And the amazing thing is that when our love is outpoured, it is not depleted. The more we give, the more we have to give. It is renewed from the great reservoir of God's love which is inexhaustible.

And when we are longing to pour out the love of God that possesses us, He will provide the channel. It may be to our spouse, our child, our neighbor, one who is alone, or bereaved, or old. Recently I saw on a bumper sticker, "Love is ageless." That teenager, that man in the nursing home, that wife shut in with the sick husband. These must be the objects of our outpoured love.

And love is persistent. It doesn't give up though rebuffed, or disappointed, or unappreciated. Love seeks not her own. Tolerance grows when love is outpoured. Love covers a multitude of sins.

Love ministers to the body, but it also ministers to the spirit.

Love accepts another just as he is.

Love does not sit in judgment on another.

Love does not say or listen to unkind things about another.

Love does not take or purposely give offense.

Love seeks to understand another.

Love bears another's burdens in prayer.

Erma Bombeck was asked recently what she would do if she had her life to live over. Among other things she said, "I would have cried and laughed less while watching television . . . and more while watching real life. There would have been more I love yous . . . more I'm sorrys . . . more I'm listenings."

I think she was saying, "There would be a lot more outpoured love."

No more telling illustration of outpoured love is to be found in all literature than that recorded in Mark 14. As Jesus was being entertained in the home of Simon the leper, a woman, unnamed by Mark but probably Mary, sister of Martha and Lazarus, came with an alabaster jar of very expensive perfume. Its cost would represent a year's wages. Breaking the seal, she poured the precious ointment on the head of Jesus. It was an act of extravagant, uncalculating love.

Its effect was immediate and striking. Among those who witnessed the display arose the harsh and indignant protest, "What a waste! What misappropriation of funds! How insensitive to the needs of the poor!" And most horrifying of all, it was evidently the final straw that brought Judas Iscariot to the point of betrayal. The record states that he then sought out the chief priests and arranged to sell his Lord into their hands for money.

But the effect of this outpouring of love upon Jesus himself was in sharp contrast. He rebuked the protest and described the act as "beautiful," and further declared that it would immortalize the woman who had so lavishly outpoured her love upon Him.

Where do our hidden sympathies lie? With the betrayer, or with the one who demonstrated supreme and unrestrained affection? The Master said, "She hath done what she could." Have we done *all* that we could to demonstrate unbounded love to Christ our Savior and Redeemer?

12

Take MYSELF, and I will be Ever, only, all for Thee.

For Thee, that is the beginning and the end of consecration.

The Son of God loved me and gave himself for me. Out of the realization of the *for me* inevitably comes the total *for Thee*. This is the complete offering up of self, the whole personality—hands, feet, voice, mind, will, possessions, emotions—all totally yielded.

The consecration is total in its *constancy*. It is to be *ever*. No drawing back. No recounting of the cost. No lack of enthusiasm. Thoroughly, irrevocably committed. All out!

The consecration is total in its *exclusiveness*. It is to be *only*. No other Master. No distractions. No wavering of allegiance. He and He alone. The compass needle of the soul pointing always in one direction.

The consecration is total in its *completeness*. It is to be *all*. My entire being at His disposal. No reservations. No withholdings. No bargaining. Utterly, wholly His own.

Constantly, exclusively, completely His—ever, only, all for Thee.